TELLING TALES

From A Corner Of Lancashire

MARIANNA MICHELL

With illustrations by Harold Gosney

Q

First Published in Great Britain in 2023 by
Quacks Books
7 Grape Lane, Petergate, York, YO1 7HU
Tel: +44 (0)1904 635967
Email: design@quacks.info
Website: radiusonline.info
Quacks Books is an Imprint of Radius Publishing Ltd

Copyright © Marianna Michell 2023
Illustrations © Harold Gosney 2023

The moral right of Marianna Michell and Harold Gosney to be identified as the author and illustrator respectively of this work has been asserted in accordance with the Copyright, Designs and Patents Act of 1988.

All rights reserved. No part of this publication may be reproduced, stored in a retrieval system, or transmitted in any form or by any means, electronic, mechanical, photocopying, recording, or otherwise, without the prior permission of both the copyright owner and the above publisher of this book.

A CIP catalogue record for this book is available from the British Library.

ISBN Paperback: 978-1-912728-70-1

Set in twelve point Arial with a page size of 210mm x 148mm printed by offset lithography on a one hundred gsm offset.

Contents

Arty-Barty-Bush	5
Lessons from the playground	8
"Not related"	11
Accidents happen!	16
Sweeping the old year out	19
The old shack	21
Uncle William	25
Acts of God	28
Scenting the past	30
Work and play	35
Spaces …	41
Pendle view	46

Preface

"Stop telling tales!" was the admonition if a child gossiped or sounded to be stretching the truth. In writing stories from our personal memory, the truth is subject to 'slippage'. It could be distance in time from the occasion or character: but more than that, our unconscious selects what to say, and de-selects other aspects. In this way, you may find these Tales to be 'telling' of the author's memory bias. I trust you will accept the title of this volume in that spirit.

The themes of these tales could be summarised as *Places, Faces and Spaces.* Youthful memories which prompted them returned one by one, surfacing between April 2019 and October 2022. I am grateful to Lance Edwards whose quarterly magazine *Open Views* meant I kept returning to clean pages, fingers poised! I am also grateful to Nick Morrice who set the right example for me. Just write!

A creative partnership with an imaginative illustrator, Harold Gosney has richly topped off my experience of creating this book.

Marianna Michell, York, June 2023

Arty-Barty-Bush

In my memory, he is still there with his wooden barrow and broom, always on the same corner of the lane, sweeping up leaves. A troop of children on our way up to school or down, we did not question why Arthur Barker appeared there more often than at other spots.

That spot is about half-way up the hill from Lane Bottom to Haggate School - a place with no room for a real pavement because of the wall. A copse of trees up a steep bank crowds above the wall, and darkens the path; and the base of the wall narrows it. Ah, now it's clear of course why he was often found there, brushing, and forking it all up into the barrow. Trees doing what they love to do each year would cause quite a heap at certain times. Yet time, for me, has squashed the year into a continuous fall of leaves and an ever present Arty-Barty-Bush.

I need to explain the title of my tale. The grown-ups were amused at one toddler's attempt to say, 'Arthur Barker's brush'. That was all. Odd twists of pronunciation and especially local errors like that run down like laughter for decades. For as long as people are local. Not people who have moved here and don't know things that we know.

Every day of our primary years we would plod the same route. Arthur Barker's voice was no more than a rumble from the earth. The growl meant '*ow do*? His face was very old. Out in all weathers, an old man doing that job for so many years: did anybody pay him? I understood his pause, his leaning on the broom: *Glad to talk to young'uns. Glad of other people.* But I hear now that my benign image is not the whole story. Another in our troop heard other things, *If you don't behave, I'll tell 'police on yer!* I'm left wondering if I was as deaf then as now, or did I whitewash these encounters?

Once around the corner he was forgotten, a character taken for granted. He had no parents, no wife, no children, he did not live anywhere. He was like our schoolteachers whom the youngest kids assumed must live at school. Teachers do not go to shops or go home for tea. Road sweepers only sweep roads.

School was at the very top of the hill. If it was dry weather, good; if wet, still good but we wore rubber trousers over our clothes. Marvellously unfashionable and perfectly acceptable because most of us wore them. Once in the school porch the rubber clothing was removed with whatever difficulty, along with wellies and any wet socks. We weren't supposed to climb onto the great iron radiators to get warm, but we did. We were a clan and we knew where the rules stretched to and we all played the games which kids do – until we heard the caretaker's voice. Then we would jump down and find our classrooms.

Some children had more sweets than others. After school, they seemed to go in the corner shop at the crossroads more often than I did. My weekly penny did not stretch to a stick of liquorice, but you could ask somebody if you could chew the other end of theirs for a bit. Walking back down the hill again, there were flags to walk on, all nice and wide and regular. We called them flags but I noticed later that when real stone was replaced with concrete slabs, it got called pavement.

It's only when you get to that narrow bit on the left that you walk one after the other because it's uneven. And it's shady when the leaves are hushing overhead, or it's windy and the leaves are waiting for Arthur's brush. But nobody walks on that narrow bit anymore - too many cars. Quite likely the council has removed the path altogether to widen the road. Instead, they created a safe pathway on the other side of the road, and a swathe of red colour warns drivers of possible walkers. When they created the new path, they did not remove the wall there, but put in some steps. So it's high and with a valley on the far side it can be windy, and there's a handrail.

But I don't know about that because I don't go that way. I'm still walking where memory plays the leaves into a dance, and we talk to an old man with a wooden barrow.

Lessons from the playground

'The big ship sailed through the allee-allee-oh, on the last day of September'.

It was a playground game. Like many other activities where children are together, not overseen, it was more than that. Looking back, what a success those activities were. There's a world of difference between learning in the classroom and learning in the playground. In the 1950s, what went on in the classroom was geared to the individual grasping the tools of life, but playtime was a different learning: it was about how we work with each other, how we respond, and what it said about each of us.

Do you remember this action song? Known as a 'thread-needle game', lots of children form a line, negotiating who would be the one at the wall end. She – usually she - would form an arch with one arm against the wall. The singing would start. The child at the other end would march or skip everyone through the arch and back almost to where they began, but not quite: as the last child passes under the arch, she had to twist herself around the other way. Thus, again and again we progressed through until finally we were all twisted the other way, arms akimbo. If we didn't fall over, giggling, we would then dance back-to-back on the spot.

We played Fairies and Witches. There was nothing to it really – quite disappointing. Someone else made the decisions and I was always a fairy, not dangerous at all. Why was that? And if mum had given me clogs with metal tips like my friend's, would I have kicked *her* shins, or not dared? My clogs had leather tips, so not much point!

There was less mobility in those times. People stayed put.

One wonderful result was that we girls performed the same songand-dance routines as my mother's generation had done - and in the same outdoor toilets. The floor area was L-shaped, entrance leading to a line of toilets graded in size from infant-bottoms to teacher-bottoms. Indeed! Our chorus-line of dancing girls would squash along by the toilets, agreeing on a song from our very small repertoire. Decision made, we would appear, legs kicking, across the front to a waiting crowd of cross-legged children, to sing, 'She'll be comin' round the mountain.' The whole scenario flowed down from the previous generation, featuring the American show movies of the 30s.

Playtime offered the opportunity to learn about the opposite sex. The girls' toilet block features once more. Girls were on the receiving end of pee from over the adjoining wall. Boys would be boys, in mum's generation and in ours, and the message had been the same in mum's time: 'Please Miss Ellingham, the boys are pee-ing over the toilet wall again'. 'Oh dear, girls, we'll have to tell them again, won't we?' We girls carefully delegated who would report this to one of our teachers.

I won't name names, nor is this an admission that children went AWOL, but one lunchtime a group of us sneaked out of the gate, turned right and within seconds were in the neighbouring field. Some of us were just following-my-leader as usual. I recall a brief agreement between boy and girl; something like, "I will if you will." Pants down from him and her, with other kids peering wide-eyed.

History in the classroom comprised a thick book: *The March of Time*, with pictures of Egyptians and the River Nile. Outdoors, history was much more recent: a sea-shanty dating back only 150 years! *Boney was a warrior (hey lads hey), Boney was a warrior (John Franswaa). Went to St Helena, hey lads hey....* and so on. Like all traditional songs, bits got forgotten and other bits were added, and the verses were muddled – history being mangled in the process.

But that Big Ship. Which ship, on which date and which event? The question wasn't asked. We just skipped and sang.

"Not related"

When you are too young to spell, you collect words by ear. Our neighbour to the right was called Jonet. He kept hens. His back garden spread across the far end of ours, so our fence backed onto hen-hut-view. I was once taken up there to have a look: out of our back yard across the slutchy street and up their garden to walk with the hens.

Being a terrace of seven houses, we were all linked in various ways. Our yard's party wall was very useful in one respect. We put out a bright red plastic cullender with a note in saying how many eggs we wanted and how many cracked eggs as well, with the right money. 2/6d. They were cheaper. When 'Jonet' had done our order, we'd hear a knocking on the living-room wall, so we'd go out and collect the eggs. When we ate the eggs, I would sometimes ask how we knew it was only yolk, and there wouldn't be baby chickens inside. The answer was always: "because t'cock hasn't been in wit th'en". Deep frustration on my part:
There's the hen - and there is the cock. What has it got to do with the chickens and eggs?!

Jonet Slack turned out to have a surname which was not Slack and was the same as my granny's, but mum would insist 'we aren't related'. *But if it's the same and we're in the same village, we could be related further back.* But most people aren't so interested in what has been. And life for cotton-workers was honourable but difficult. No HP for my mum and dad. Straight cash and no borrowing except your mortgage of a few hundred pounds. They just worked and held things together. The whole district, for ages past, was inter-related but it meant nothing. I grew old enough to recognise that there may be a place called Slack. *John of the Slack.* So he was not called Jonet. My friend was called

Janet. He was not Jonet, and I had worked it out. He was John.

Conversations overheard included 'Slack Farm'. He was a son of that farm. In my long forays around the countryside, I found Slack Farm. They must have had problems with moles because every so often I'd spot a wooden sign stuck in the ground by the roadside. It read

MOLE
CHAP
CALL

Nice and square, that. Three words of equal length. Simple message: *We work with muck around 'ere*, like our back street where we played the live-long day, topped up every so often with sludge but we thought the word was slutch. Slutch was ok to play in.

Now, I may be giving the impression we were one of many streets. No, our front street had the honour of being the last before a long valley. It was also 'unadopted', and remains so - offering mountainous terrain down the front street, for the occasional car or van. Our row was surrounded by fields and hills as far as Pendle Hill to the front and the Yorkshire border somewhere to the back. Farmers drove down the front street and into the valley, and the gate had to be kept shut. When it wasn't, the result was *'beeasts in t' backyard'*. Cows would mill gloomily around our kitchen window. Sometimes it was my cousin's pigs on the loose, kept perhaps in some unofficial place. Lots of unofficial events sprang from that family.

The valley is really called Walverden from the name of the brook. But it was known as t'pigole. Pig Hole Farm was the first building you came to. At one point it held a family of eight children whom I knew, all names beginning with J. After they left, it fell into disrepair and the afore-mentioned person who had pigs took to removing lead pipe-structures which ran around and from the roof. Later, this near ruin was turned into a family home by folks who shut off the stile and with it the right of way. But there was a way around, past where the pigsties were falling to further ruin, so I would walk that way feeling disgruntled - perhaps like the pigs of olden times.

Visitors to our front street, which was after all on the edge of nowhere, included the rag and bone man. At first, you just heard his shout which had corrupted over his lifespan to, "hey hoooo…." *Quick, rag an'bone man's 'ere.* The horse and cart is lumbering down the lumpy street.

Did anyone ever have bone to put in it, and if so – what sort of bone?!

The other occasional visitor was the gas-chap. Near our front steps was one of two gas-lamps for the street. Even when they all became electrified, in common speech they were still gas-lamps. The reason the posts had that horizontal protrusion at the top was so that the man could rest his ladder there to climb up and change the gas mantle. And one dusk, I saw him do just that.

We were a street which stayed put. John o't' Slack and his wife and son may have lived there longer than anyone else, but the other six houses also rarely changed ownership or tenancy. No. 27 saw the shortest stay – the final months of Auntie Annie's life. We would call it hypothermia now. We already knew her because mum took me to Annie's previous old house down by the river, with the path to the blue-bell woods, and hens scampering in the under-belly of the house. Her husband had died suddenly. They had the same surname as our cousins who had also lived at no. 27, but again mum said, "she isn't related"!

So, Auntie Annie was brought nearer to civilisation, but she couldn't get used to the notion of heating no. 27. I saw that her hands were blue, and the house was candle-lit because she didn't use the electric lights. Too long spent in a house in a valley alone by the river with only gas-light, a deer skull and antlers on the wall, and a slop-stone sink to serve as kitchen and washing area.

Later, the many families in my district revealed themselves through ancestry research, when many relationships of old fell into place. For most people, it was, and still is of little consequence to look outwards from that valley, nor backwards to where we had come from. I wandered further than most. As a child I had a recurring dream about being in a dark old house like Annie's which sloped dangerously towards a river. I was scared it might collapse. I understood later that this was my inner house: it was the mood of my upbringing, my childhood 'house' which needed slowly to collapse into a wider and more flowing river.

Accidents happen!

A tumble from your bike, a fall on the ice, a bash, a gash on the leg, splinter in the finger, little bump on the head! Life-changing injuries stay with us, but do we recall the many bumps and bruises of childhood – toddler-tumbles when you tottered indoors bawling? We were learning about life the hard way, and we measured our growing up by them.

At first, we expected everybody to pay attention: *Help!* Later, we learned to mop up our hurts and the scrapes we got into. The first bump I recall went like this: I'm on daddy's shoulders and he's walking through the back yard, stepping towards the back door and I see a stone lintel coming towards my forehead (I didn't know the word lintel of course). And you guessed it... *Help!*

From mum, "Nay, Jack! 'ad yer forgotten shi wer on yer showders?"

Another dad-mistake was when he decided to show me where he went rabbit-shooting. It isn't far he said – I was to follow him behind his greenhouse full of red tomatoes, and into the field over the barbed-wire fence. *Help! He's taller than me and I've taken a lump out of my leg!* I don't recall much fuss at home, though I think the rabbit shooting event was curtailed. And it healed over fine – I started to feel proud of the little wounds and their ability to heal over – that triangular memento from barbed-wire is so faint now.

We kids played in the front field, by clambering over the wall straight across from our front door - naughty to do that but we didn't mess it up too much and no-one told us not to. Why I was crouching down in a hollow I don't know, but a lad my age, 12, started hammering on my spine with his fists! Well, I didn't stop to ponder the potential injury, but straightened up and socked him one with my lefty clenched fist. Blood ran from his nose and a wail from his mouth. And my middle finger hurt. *Help!* Indoors, but this time there was no response from mum or dad to my proclamation "Look, my finger's bent!" But now I'm old and I still play the piano even with a bent finger, so I must let them off I suppose.

My home-made wooden sledge with rope threaded through two holes at the front, had seen a lot of action. This time, my trusty sledge saw the chain-link fence coming up at the bottom of the hill as it skewed from the expected line, and I saw it too - but there were no brakes on this mode of travel, and nothing to stop me from sliding at great speed, knees first, into the fence.

My left knee hurt a lot as I dragged the sledge and myself back over the wall and indoors. *Help!* It was a neat red cut all across my knee-cap, "like a mouth", someone said. Nice. Over the weeks, it healed very well, and I must have avoided picking the scab because the scar faded and is now gone. Oh, what a shame – nothing to show for that 'deep' experience. Years later, mum said that when I rolled up my trouser legs and bent my knee to show them, she could see the bone...

But the question I want to ask is, "As a child, do you recall the first time you got hurt but decided not to cry?"

Sweeping the old year out

I don't go in for New Year's resolutions - if there are changes it's because I'm ready and willing to change something. Despite that, one bright New Year's Eve a few years ago, I found myself wielding the long-handled duster, 'de-cobwebbing' from ceiling to floor. I was well into it, when it sprang to mind what I would have done as a youngster at home in Lancashire, on New Year's Eve. It's called 'sweeping the old year out' and this is how it would go.

In preparation, the family needs to make sure the fire has been out for some time, so that the soot along the back of the grate is not hot. Some form of fat (mum would have done it and I expect it was lard) is spread all over your face; the soot is then applied as evenly as possible. Afterwards, a form of disguise is applied - dad's hat, old trousers and jacket. To sweep, of course, you need a brush and shovel (most folk now say 'dustpan and brush' but that was too posh), then the little troupe of mummers is ready for off - don't forget the box or can for money!

Perhaps in the distant past, the tradition would entail a performance of some kind, long ago lost, but all we knew was that on a dark and chilly New Year's evening, we moved from door to door throughout the whole village and up the hill, humming loudly outside each house. If they didn't hear, we would knock at the door as well. At some doors, the occupants would be familiar with the custom, and humming had the desired effect of bringing to the door a smiling and expectant face - you would be let in and, still humming confidently would go about cleaning up. No-one minded at all. I'm talking of the 1960s, so most people in a Lancashire village would still have open fires. This would mean a modest amount of dust, or ashes anyway, enough to make you feel you were doing a real job, before they popped a threepenny bit in the can. I got used to being peered at with comments such as 'Jack's daughter in't it?' to which I tried not to grin.

But the tradition was on its last legs, and it stopped when my friends and I stopped. We had performed this custom for perhaps three years, no doubt following many generations before us, but I saw that one terraced cottage after another was occupied by 'new people'. I'm sure they were local enough, but it didn't feel so - and they didn't all welcome us. The final year, we foolishly spent too long knocking and humming at a door, determined to get in! Eventually a young girl, apparently a baby-sitter, came to the door and spoke angrily, "Get lost, yer mummish nits, yer'v woken t'baby"! That did it. The language was restrained by present day levels, and I noted that she recognised us as mummers, but somehow, we never went round again.

The old shack

Why does absence make the heart grow fonder? Absence of someone is one thing, but absence of places may seem strange and introverted. It's memory of buildings that really gets me. I write of these spaces because the buildings enfold youthful memories. Now they are dismantled and removed. Felled like trees. Some may remain, but I am not around to know.

Yes, sometimes the characters in their landscape, their voice, their unique form, or gait, become memory's focus. But I have spaces in my mind where the buildings of my childhood and youth are visible. One of these was discovered by my cousin Steven and myself when I was about 11 and he 9. I have always identified Steven as 'my cousin', yet clearly, with respect to this tale, he was my best friend.

Steven and his elder brother, with their parents, moved house suddenly every few years. Well, that's how it seemed. Old farm cottages would serve for a few years, then it's a move – only across the field perhaps. I can still smell the old damp stone and crumbling mullions of the house they lived in at this time. It was one of two – the larger cottage next door remaining vacant for years: they were farmer and assistant's cottages. The date on the larger cottage, 1822, I identified later as the year when my idol Percy Shelley died off the coast of Italy; and now two centuries have passed since the cottages were topped off with their date.

On the road outside, the lads played footie, voicing the gasps of their imaginary stadium crowd. The occasional car or farm-van never broke the spell. It was a simple stepaside and then get back in. Our male cousins, so much taller than we were, dashed about or stood poised with foot extended waiting to receive the ball. And beyond them stands Hill Farm, empty then, with pig-sties we investigated for a possible den. Too low for us.

On a foray only one field away, we spot from the road an old hut. Interested, we cross the field, and peering underneath we find old bones! This had to be significant and sinister. It was inconceivable that we should come to a logical conclusion: that this was a disused hen-hut from the time great uncle William lived at the neighbouring Holt Hill Farm, and therefore these are the bones of dead hens. No! this is suspicious - and from that moment, it was our place, *Bony Shack!*

Back home, a flag is created. It is painted in black and white, and I learn that 'skull and cross bows' is actually 'skull and cross-bones'. Much skill is gained by working out how to string the flag in a way that allows us to haul the flag up and down to indicate when we are in residence. Rather than using the ruined door to the hut, we adopt a mode of entry and exit on the near-side, by discovering a rectangular gap close to the floor, which we enlarge. Ingeniously, access is obtained via a sliding mechanism whereby a small blackboard from home has become our door.

Bony Shack is in two parts: section A is in good shape, but section B always needs repairs. There is a deal of nail-banging. A system of glass-jars showing varieties of nail, hangs from the ceiling. Later, we install a heating system: a fire-container with some piping above it. We assume it's safe…I have no memory of its operation, but I acknowledged that by around 11, Steven seemed to know about such things. Once, a friend requests slices of bacon from her mother, with bread, and bacon butties are enjoyed.

Matches were not left there due to damp. And damp was

the fate of the lump of carpet we lugged in, offering our first experience of the smell of mould. Small gaps in section B's fragile end wall created a look-out position. Just once, lads from a nearby new-build (much despised) were seen coming over the wall towards us. It was disappointing after that, that they did not return. We kept looking…

The field was sometimes occupied by more than ourselves, and these were quadrupeds. We did not mind bullocks as we knew they were frisky but not necessarily a danger. Bony Shack was a distance from the road and visible from there so, upon arrival at the lane-end, we could always see if we had a small herd to pass through. One time, we passed confidently amongst them only to become enveloped in warm, sweaty, young male bovines. We quickened our pace (as the stories always describe it) and accelerated towards the shack. No time to slide open the low door so we leapt on the roof - and it did not give way! Exultant, there we remained until the bullocks lost interest.

Playing out was normal and without danger, and external doors were not locked so we came and went. "A' yer goin' up to Bony?" was mum's question, often. Childhood excitement matured into wonder. As I grew up, walking for miles became a liberation from a restrictive adult atmosphere of which I was only half-conscious. In the early evenings I learnt to take a poetry book with me - though listening and watching swallows flying through the broken doorway was too enchanting to pay attention to my book. This was an emotional time as I sought the loveliness of the world and of the arts. But an act of betrayal brought the end of childhood.

That final time, there was no view of Bony Shack from the road. I peered up the field in disbelief and plodded sadly forwards. A fire had consumed our old refuge. None of our stuff was left there at all and I returned home to tell everyone. I was told that a maiden-aunt had got it removed because as we were now older, "all sorts of things could happen that shouldn't". I could not have imagined a narrower interpretation of the times we had spent there. She lived nearby, and close to Holt Hill Farm where our great uncle had lived and worked. After his death, she had felt responsible.

Hitherto, she had been an innocent elderly aunt but to our minds was so no longer. It was unjust. Steven aged around 12 might have continued the loving round of repairs to its structure for some time to come, but I had to grow into a young adult. The tomboy had to evolve – but that's another story.

Uncle William

Memories are tainted. What I think I know may be corrected tomorrow by a friend, asking, "Don't you remember?" Uncle William, likely the keeper of the hens in my previous tale, was my great uncle and the unmarried uncle of my mother. One of a line of Nuttalls in Briercliffe, near Burnley, so numerous as tenant farming chaps at the time, that the term *'Nuttle breed'* was spoken.

Mum told me of one encounter with Uncle William. As a child, she had set off for a walk across the fields and, just as I did a generation later, she passed through Uncle William's front yard. One day she heard his voice somewhere in a dark little hovel to the left. "Hiya, our Ida!" There he was, in a murky outhouse perched on his toilet, trousers round his ankles and legs outspread supporting a newspaper. Of course, he needed sunlight to read by, so why close the door?

I knew his brother, my grandad, a little better. As an infant I must have sat on his knee at times because mum reported a kind observation I made. "Grandad – your hair has gone off – but never mind 'cos it's comin' out of ya ears." I was not to know until so many years later, about marital rape of my grandma, the crying heard through the wall by mum and her sister. In her old age, mum reported to me he had been a 'peeping Tom'. But what of his brother William? Should we suspect him too? My memory is limited by youth but I believe not otherwise tainted or inaccurate. First, it's a memory of a farm-house with what to me was a grand portico. Allegedly, this had contained a priest-hole.

From daylight I step into darkness. It's a stone porch with great coats hanging above me on the left, muffling all footsteps on the flag floor, then a door to the right into his living-room. Another flag floor, and there's nothing to light up the gloom except a single window. On some visits, it's a warm space, and perhaps there's a lamb on either side of the big fireplace: the ewe their mother would have died, and he feeds them himself from a bottle.

I sit down and Uncle William is to my left, seated and smiling in an ancient wooden rocking chair. I have just two memories of these visits. The clearest is the invitation, "Does ta want an 'umbug?" Every visitor hears this and usually accepts the offer. The humbug hampers speech but then we stare into the fire as we struggle through the mint. And I mustn't forget the Dandelion and Burdock. Unfamiliar with that? It's a fiery herbal drink, the production of it recently revived.[1]

In his age he often repeated with a chuckle: "Nobody knows what I 'ave under my arse!" I would hear this with discomfort. I didn't want to think about his arse! His death in the mid-1960s revealed cash under the seat - around £6000. I wondered then if money and humbugs had got mixed up; after all, he only raised his bulk from the chair long enough to retrieve the bag.

His generation - and the following, are all now 'gathered unto their fathers.' We cousins are numerous but dwindling. I wonder how far their versions of these stories might differ from mine.

Where does the truth lie?

---

[1] https://mrfitzpatricks.com

Acts of God

I don't remember what time of year it was, but I think of it as July. It was another day passing quietly into history, but the speed of events fixed it forever. It's like a movie I can summon to mind over and over.

One moment it was summer. Then "darkness covered the face of the earth", quickly enough to pull people to their front doors to strain their eyes upwards. "It's like th'end o't world cummin!" called someone a couple of doors down, as we witnessed the most disturbing view of a silent, heaving black sky. As we peered upwards, from the blackness came one, then two then many lethally large stones of ice. In the gathering tumult, there was a general retreat indoors away from that enormous racket - in the yard, on the windows, the roof, against the doors.

From each front room, neighbours peered from our valley up the green hill. The summit above us, piled with rapidly melting ice glistened for a second then spilt its shining load downwards like a bursting dam. Halfway down the hill, two walls at right-angles held the gathering lake only briefly, then the top-stones – each maybe four feet in length, were swept away. Meanwhile, unseen water adding to the surface water sank to the valley floor so that, there in front of us, an underground stream gushed its load up through stone and soil to surprise us with a waterspout, then another and another, revealing a water-table some had never guessed was there. A field where we kids played each day had become a line of geysers spreading down the valley.

We call it a wonder of nature, or an act of God. In the past, such a sky would portend misfortune: punishment for transgression. We would attribute great meaning to unexplained events, and we still struggle for explanations - picking events apart, to analyse, reduce, deduce. I still wonder how deeply underground, or near the surface, was that watertable.

The mind has such depths, too. And we still ourselves to know, to learn - but the wonder remains.

Scenting the past

I had a dream, where a track down from a main road just might lead to that farm we visited as children. Down the track, indeed, was the farm where childhood memories lay. In the dream, somehow I was not surprised when we came upon it as a ruin, and though the walled tracks close by did not fit the scene I had remembered, I still felt hopeful this was the same spot.

When I woke up, I was tempted to look up the family we had known. If I mention that the parents' first and surnames all began with B and they were from Blackburn, you may conclude they were caricatures from a TV soap, but no! My mother and Betty B were bridesmaids for each others' weddings. Betty B married Brian B. Their girls worked on the farm from a young age, and we stayed there for periods of time for haymaking. My dad helped Brian. There was no combine-harvester. It was forks and trailers, and no bails but heaps of fabulous-smelling hay for us kids to climb and to romp in. In the barn, we heard the rats and mice but didn't see any, so sliding down and messing up the pile held no fears.

As in another tale here, this dairy farm comprised two adjoining cottages, the family living at first in the smaller one, with the main cottage empty. We four girls were aged between 5 and 11 at this point, and the farming sisters already had jobs: they were entrusted with the sizing up of eggs! That dairy room was off the living kitchen with its flag floor, and an old workhorse table with what was termed 'grand-piano legs' wrapped around by cloths. Somewhere I learnt that Victorians covered shapely table legs in case they encouraged sexy thoughts. In 1961, the legs were still covered….

The other room was the parlour, very compact and likewise flag-floored, but with a fireplace - though I don't remember a fire in the grate - and a sofa. A rag rug attempted in vain to warm up the stone floor, and a grandfather clock spooked me with its sun and moon faces: symbols of night and day. I peered at their silent, imperceptible turning as if fearing they were alive. This parlour was near the bottom of the stairs, and by the unused front-door which led only to the cow-churned lane of mud and cow-dung. We only ever ventured across the lane to reach the toilet, in a tiny hut accessed first by a stile, then a perilous jumble of stones. Cow-dung, a stile, stones, and darkness. A challenge for someone in a hurry!

Those of us old enough to have breathed gas anaesthetic at the dentist can still smell it in our minds. It's often said that of all our senses, that of smell is the first to be recalled. And so, outdoors at the farm, it was the cow-pat smell, familiar to anyone living in a pastoral landscape - yet I associate those visits with the smell of damp stone. How can hard stone absorb damp? But, in an unheated space, everything remains tinged with damp. The family must have been used to it, but as a child I had an uneasy sense, as if cold and damp retains a scent of the past. The family moved later to the empty house next door, a big step up for a young farming couple, and suddenly they had an enormous bathroom, and the damp smell was less pervasive.

Perhaps my interest in 'what lies beneath' mossy masonry, water-worn stone-flags, and the scent of centuries began there in the 1950s, but it was further excited when watching the TV film, *The Stone Tapes* which was aired in 1972. Based upon the concept of residual memory in a building, something like this phenomenon occurred in my life in recent times. We might say that a building remembers, though some maintain that we experience a timeslip. Reports given by workmen as they created Jorvik Viking Centre in York, talked of witnessing the march of Roman soldiers; that occurrence points in the same direction as my experience.

I was renting a house near York after living abroad. My household on the high seas was about to catch up with me, so I rented a spacious old house to allow for sifting and sorting through boxes. This was a late Victorian former police house which had been replaced by a modern dwelling forty years previously. The old house had become unsaleable due to increased traffic, being yards from one of the busiest roads in the county, with juggernauts passing several times a minute.

As you enter the main door, you step into a hallway with the kitchen to the left, a heavy wooden door ahead, leading to the 'prison corridor'. The door's enormous, black-painted iron bolt is testimony to its former purpose. Beyond that door, the corridor leads to another door above which remains an iron-barred window, evidence of one of the two cells. Petty criminals only, I was assured. It helped a little to be told so!

Over the next few months, two strange events happened in the house. One morning I awoke hearing a familiar sound: a loose carpet grip on the landing jangled as if trodden on. My eyes popped open to see a young man walk briskly through the closed door, adjusting all the while the small collar of his short shirt. He stopped a foot or so to my right and seemed to be checking in a mirror, perhaps of a wardrobe which was no longer there. I sensed, 'He doesn't know you are here'. For a few seconds, therefore, I scanned a slim young man with short dark hair, a white shirt which ended or was tucked in at the waist, and dark trousers. He was close enough to touch, and then he was gone. Later, I would tell myself, 'no spirit but residual memory - a repeat of a daily action', as if I had tapped into a previous period in the life of the house. After this, I made subtle inquiries locally about young men who had lived there in recent generations, and none were known. Quite possibly I had glimpsed a young policeman preparing for his day, but from how far back in time, I don't know.

The second unexplained event, some weeks later, was fleeting. I stepped from the entrance hall to my right, and stepping through the opening, my left hand moved behind me as if to close a door. There was no door to close. I examined the frame and noted that the profile of the door jambs was different from other such entrances which had never had doors. I could see that hinges had been present but the indents had been filled in and painted. It seemed that I had shared a memory of a door which was no longer there. Others had shut that door as a matter of course, and I was sharing their atmosphere. If that is so, then it seems that a building may influence our actions.

Like all dreams, my dream of the track to the farm ruin is my own task to understand. We step forward while integrating memories which have made us who we are. We assume we are in the present time and yet, the scent of a more distant past lingers.

Work and Play

Both photographs had been taken in exactly the same place, around fifteen years apart. That was serendipitous, and I don't know who took the more recent one. It was touching to consider all that had happened in between. The first photo was in black and white while the later one, in colour, showed children I did not know, skipping around a Maypole. But the date of the colour photo had connotations which were grey and not at all dance-like.

It felt like a miracle when the first photo reappeared after all those years. We sisters seated on the old trolley-cart were squinting into the sunlight with eager expressions. This was the only photo of the treasured vehicle which had trundled up and down the village streets, until I as its owner recognised that even a grown-up tomboy must give in - and give it away! Behind us in the photo are the flattened remains of the cotton mill.

An outsider would see only some colourless desert - a wasteland of dust and stone, but what children can make of such a space! The old mill site, untended after demolition, created a wonderland for wheels of all kinds. Roller-skates for one child, tricycle for another, bicycle if you were a lucky one! Best of all, the trolley, even if someone had to push you and you steer with your feet, or they pull the rope – *don't go too fast or I'll fly off on a corner…*

Motorways were created! Clearing the way for another motorway meant sweeping. A long-handled brush was borrowed from home but later was returned, bristles flat and ready only for the bin. Boulders of unknown origin as big as armchairs and many times heavier couldn't be shifted and so became landmarks. And no local authority had come to warn us of the dangers from bent metal protruding from these great lumps. The only time I ever had a black eye was when we took to skimming chunks of thick and crumbling wall plaster and I got one in the eye socket. Did they put asbestos in the mix of that plaster, or fibreglass - or were these things not heard of in 1848?

1848. In our district of Briercliffe, handloom weavers still clacked away in Mr. William Smith's three-storey Hill Factory whilst around the corner, their offspring learnt the new ways at his Hill End Mill, one of the earliest steam-driven powerloom cotton mills in the area.[2] New power from steam matched spinning with the new water-frame of Arkwright. A village was not the usual place for a shed of four-hundred looms but the spring-line from the hill saw Mr. Smith use that factor to keep the trade going, both for himself and for the locals. The youngest came in as cotton-piecers: picking up fragments for re-use. Teenagers managed steam-driven looms. The experienced came in from afar as over-lookers, and to keep the engines hot.

---

[2] https://en.wikipedia.org/wiki/Harle_Syke_Mill

And so, a village in a valley, with stone houses built for workers, slowly blackened with smoke. Even after the Reform Act and the start of co-operative groups, times were lean, and people were hungry for that work. In 1848 across Europe, the same depression turned to anger but not always to reform. Cities smouldered, but the old order remained.

The mill – or shed, pronounced 'shade', and its chimney were still standing well over a century after the first racket of looms started up, but metal gates across the mill's great doors never opened in our time. From the lane, we could wobbly-walk the fence running by the spinning shed and count the identical windows, each with its hypnotic 'WILFUL DAMAGE' warning. Built at a depth below the road, this meant we were on a level with its first floor and at a risky stretch from those windows. On a damp winter's evening the building was a still presence.

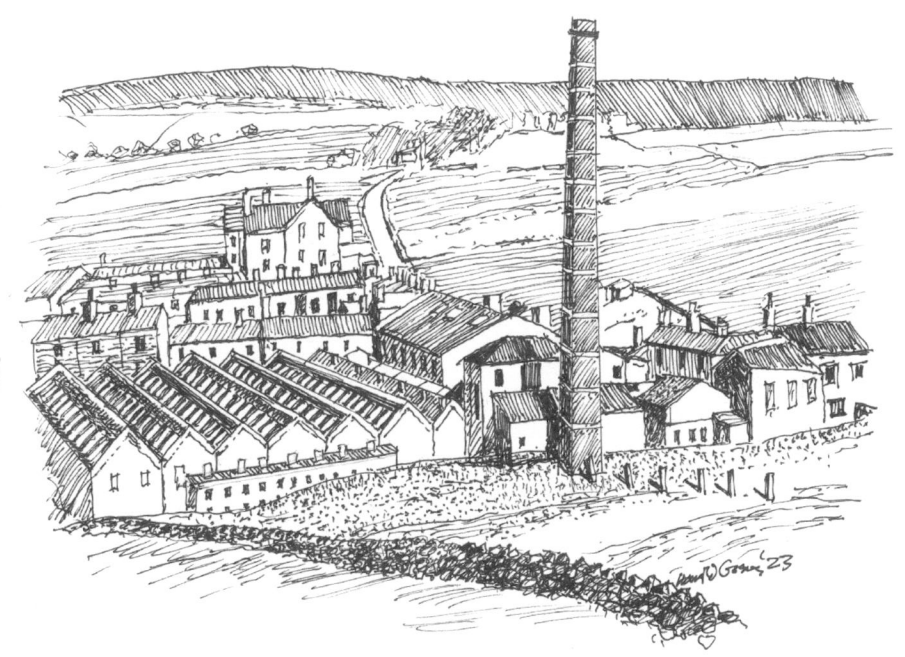

Then it was months of slow demolition and being kept off. What went first, the spinning shed with its hundreds of cones? Known in the past as 'cheeses' due to their shape when full of yarn, we stacked the empty cones into each other and flung them about. A den of labour had become a playground for us kids. Or did the weaving shed come down first? There's no clear memory, except for what was left after the main demolition: the chimney. Square-stacked and banded for strength; silent, smokeless, and very tempting for local lads. I stood scared as they lit a fire at the base of the chimney – now exposed and accessible. Everyone said come and look up inside. One second, maybe two then I backed off. *Somebody would tell us off. Or it might fall down.* Then yes – or was it wishful-thinking - standing well back and seeing smoke wisps emerge from the top?

From our parents' bedroom window, the mill site was to the left; the view directly ahead was of Pendle Hill, sublime in the sunset. Craning our necks to the right, down the wooded valley lies Nelson, visible then only as a forest of mill-chimneys. We thought we counted thirty but twice as many mills existed at one time. One of the earliest to go up – as early as 1837 - by 1964 our chimney had to come down. The steeplejack and his team ordered everyone indoors. Preparation had to be meticulous. He had explained that, though the chimney was not surrounded by houses, a too-quick shift would separate and lengthen the structure as it came down. That could send stone through windows on our street, at great force.

We weren't going to miss the great event, so our family had lunch at the front room window, perched around the Singer sewing machine. First it was removal of stone from the base where once we kids had loitered with matches, then insertion of wooden stands in exact position, then fire or small explosion to burn them away. The process unfolded hour after hour. We were too distant to see these details.

So will it happen, where will it fall, will it work? Then at last a movement… a shift of weight… The chimney loses its footing, sinks to its knees and in a great din, unfolds like a black carpet of stone over the shed-floor. Not a stone flew. Lads naively rushed to claim the copper rod from the top. "Nay lads, that's my right as the 'jack'" I do wonder if that voice was the late Fred Dibnah, veteran of all things steam, grease, and moving cogs.

In no time at all, Nelson also vanished from view as the chimney-forest beyond the valley, was cleared. Stack after stack went. In the 1960s, King Cotton had emigrated to Egypt and my father was left shaking his head: *Rubbish they're bringin' in, and we've no work left!* But for mill-workers there was a lingering and for a spell, dad and I shared mill-life when he got me a job on a double-day shift. And so for the summer weeks it was dad's motor-bike for a 6am, or a 2pm start: He to his mill, I to mine. 8 hours. People mimed to each other across the roar; or shouted directly with cupped hands into your ear. After my first day, it was cotton wool in my ears and a hairband to keep them in. On Fridays at 10pm, always there came a moment when I sensed *we're shutting down!* Weavers went about their set checking each loom then shutting off. I listened as with a religious ritual. *Over there she's shutting down; and another one gone. Going – going - silence.*

There's that second photograph somewhere. Ah yes, the coloured one of the Maypole dancing on the site of the mill. Dad had passed away aged 51 on my birthday, and within days, someone happened to give me the photo. A too-happy snap of a May Day dance played tricks with memory and pain. Children on a smooth carpark were Maypole-skipping over the bones of its past. And nearby, deep under a newly created garden, the ghost of the spinning mill.

Spaces ….

Of all the farms in that district, Jerusalem Farm seemed ominous, enticing. Visible across the valley from the highest point of the ridge, the farmhouse was no more than an outline by that time. We cannot say how quickly the stones had been scavenged for wall-repair or for new buildings, because those who knew the final occupants, or recalled what year they left, are also gone.

There's a story about the brothers who worked the farm. Alone for months on end, from time to time they would stock up on food basics which they could not raise themselves. And so it was they arrived at a corner shop in Lane Bottom, one of only two shops serving the area.

We'll ev a sack o' meyl.
"Yer can't 'av an ole sack! Weer's yer ration cards?"
Ration cards?
"Aye, don't yer know the's a war on?"
Wot waar?

That was the story I would hear as a child. Was it the first war, or the second of which they lived in ignorance? The ruins were referred to as 'Jerr, even decades later as if the farm still existed; and the shop story was still told. How distant in time do events need to be, to become the past and recognised as such? Stories take on their own life. With increased mobility, we lose these stories, and with it the ongoing culture of a place and people. We may lose it from living memory, but I believe these spaces hold their own memory, that there is no time nor space at all between them and us. In childhood I would reluctantly assume my thoughts to be only fanciful, but now? Quantum theory, dare I say, supports my intuition.

From time to time, I would walk or cycle from Lane Bottom both to stare across the valley to 'Jerr, or to explore further afield. The route was all uphill but worth it for the return journey. This roadway leads to the moors and the Yorkshire border, then - and now perhaps - an unmarked county transition; unmarked except in its effect. Views change dramatically at the top, as the pastoral landscape turns to moorland and heather. The boundary forms the highpoint of any journey between Burnley and Heptonstall, then down into Hebden Bridge.

Just as mysterious as Jerusalem Farm are the remains of 'New House', around the bend from the ridge where I would stare over the valley. The stone archway of 'New House' becomes visible from a corner where you choose either the Trawden direction, or the moors. Mysteriously alone, a monument to the past stands in the middle of a field. Approaching the stone arch, we realise it formed the entrance to a former large dwelling. It was known in my time as either 't new airse,' (the new house) or 'purs airse', (purse house). Let's look at New House – at age 18, I did so in awe! The carved lettering of the enormous stone laid flat on the grass became etched in my mind. *My Around Briercliffe* pictorial map of the area words it thus:

*"Robert Parker and Jane his wife, Robert and Henry their sonnes built this hous. May 2nd 1672". That's what it says. My memory carried with it the year 1606. Whichever is correct, New House has not been new for 350 years, but I remember it still referred to as such. Did anyone ever question the name as they uttered it, I wondered.

How about the alternative name, Purs Airse? With no firm guide except imagination, I hear it as said in its own day as "Parker's House". Later generations would forget the Parkers and speak of the building as they heard it said by the older generation: a more cursory reference, diminished over the generations until we arrive at "Purs….." Is this why more recent documents refer to it as Purse House? Has time morphed its original name, and forgotten the man Parker, with all his achievements? And what might he think of that? Curiosity prompts imagination.

The house backs onto moorland, often referred to as Boulsworth Hill, though rightly, from the valley we see Red Spar. I would sit on the fringe of these wilder lands, silent, with the most inspiring view I ever found in my life: a small Pendle Hill because so distant, with a glorious vale filling the space between. I took my seat by a mound in which I fancied was a dead chief, buried seated upright with the best view anyone can take to the next world. My position, gazing across the scene, mimicked his. The greater mound further to my right was a barrow. I have never learnt otherwise, so imagination again fills the space.

Buildings come and go. A new respect for the past led our local authorities to cease their habit of tearing down historic buildings without a glance to their past. My last lamented space is in Lane Bottom. We children on our way down the hill from Haggate School had a tradition of rounding a bend where, at the bottom of the hill the old mill faced us with its rows of blank eyes. We would shout down the hill to hear the echo of our own voices.

Hill Factory dated from 1777. Unlike its descendent, 'our' 1848 Hill End Mill which was demolished in the 1960s, Hill Factory had been built for local handloom weavers to work in, each having their own window and a large wooden loom. Quaintly, there's a reason why the old row of houses next to the mill was known as Cop Row. A bobbin of spun yarn is also known as a 'cop'. Spinning was often done at home, and in this case, home was the low terraced row right by Hill Factory. These and other scraps of history remained in the building for us to kick and chuck around.

In the 1960s, Hill Factory was bulldozed and replaced by a Police-House, so with sad irony we might say the space was suitable only for a cop-shop! Later, that was sold as a private home. But what sounds might still be heard there, where formerly the airy space around it was once occupied by a busy three-storey mill? What we see in the here-and-now is just today's incarnation of a space with its own memory.

Around Briercliffe was produced by Briercliffe Parish Council, and was the work of the Briercliffe Art Group, May 1992.

(The author is happy to be corrected as to her knowledge of the history of Briercliffe.)

Pendle View…

Pendle View is the name of at least one home in a development which doubled the size of our village in the mid '60s. Yes, I'm sure they could see Pendle Hill from the field which was torn up to make way for their intrusive new homes – as I saw them in my teens. But I doubted anyone would relish those scenes of beauty more than I. The newcomers were bound to be townies and have no special interest in the village they had messed up by coming to live in it.

In any case, we on Walverden Road had the best view of Pendle - pronounced Penl - with a green view sweeping up from the valley. I drew that view when I was 18. Minus stone walls, it looks the same now, says a friend after a visit to her cousin. The cousin and husband married around 1965 and bought the house next door to us. They have not moved house since. Is it the ageless stone which makes people remain close to the bone, or perhaps a pride in 'being local'; or is it simply the view of Pendle?

Our neighbour on the other side, known locally as John o' Slack,[3] got an article in the local paper: 'Country air good for the brain?' or some such title. John was a farmer's son; he and his wife had a son who attained a Doctorate. My sister and I later gained Masters. Next door but three, an MA likewise. Lad at the bottom house also has a Doctorate. Country air indeed - on three sides, our row was surrounded by greenery, the last outpost before a half-hour walk to Nelson through Walverden valley. But we loathed our village name, *Lane Bottom*. How uncouth. But there was something about that spot, because those seven houses rarely changed hands.

But there's a name which is worse, because ten minutes down the valley is t'Pig'ole. No, it's not a transcription from another language. Pigole. Hole for Pigs. The entire valley might once have been pig-ridden. My mother, called Ida, would tell me about her friend, also called Ida. This Ida had the surname Pighills. They lived at Pighole Farm. She told my mother: *A lad shows an interest, 'So, what's your name then?' With a sigh, I say 'Ida Pighills of Pighole Farm!'*

As kids, we wandered down to poke about the deserted pigsties. I blame my once-removed cousins for the crumbling of the barn and farm. After the farmers and their family of eight kids moved away, these lads nicked lead from the roof. Many such farms vanished into the ground, with or without ill treatment, but Pighole Farm was later renovated and reoccupied. Though I'm glad it still stands, I am a Victor Meldrew: hunching my shoulders, I grizzle about 'those newcomers who take on old farms *just to do them up and live there!*' as if they have no right to make improvements in their lives. They are bound to be lovely people really, but they are living in a region which I still love, and I am far away.

---

[3] (See 'Not Related').

No matter how far I have travelled and how old I become, I still linger in that childhood village, and still respond to the word 'Pennine' with a sense of home. I remember reading a magazine entitled *Pennine Views* and so, identifying strongly with its title, Tales like this were sent. Writing is a way to look both ways, to make some sense of who we were, to look at who we are, and to prepare to follow twists in the road ahead.

And here, we might say, is the twist in the tales I tell. Here is a musician now compelled to write about her early years: the faces, places and perhaps most significantly, the spaces - where buildings have been bulldozed or fallen to ruin; where pre-historic barrows have been imagined, and where previous occupants were seen again by some trick of space and time.

* * * *

My Tales have covered the geographical area near Burnley, known as Briercliffe and Extwistle. The scent of my ancestry has been strongest here. In some cases, family members have shown themselves at their worst, yet I still search for the best. Memory tugs at us; it retreats and is rediscovered, moulded, and twisted beyond our knowing. I may give a title such as "Pendle View". But it is after all, my memory – my view.

My drawing of Pendle Hill, 1969